SRA

Open Court Reading

Decodable Takehome Books

Level B Set 1
Books 1–40

A Division of The McGraw-Hill Companies

Columbus, Ohio

SRA/McGraw-Hill

A Division of The **McGraw·Hill** *Companies*

Printed in the United States of America.

Send all inquiries to:
SRA/McGraw-Hill
8787 Orion Place
Columbus, OH 43240-4027

ISBN 0-02-683927-X
    12 13 14 15 16 17 18 19 QPD 05 04 03

Contents

About the Decodable Takehome Books

The *SRA Open Court Reading Decodable Books* allow your students to apply their knowledge of phonic elements to read simple, engaging texts. Each story supports instruction in a new phonic element and incorporates elements and words that have been learned earlier.

The students can fold and staple the pages of each *Decodable Takehome Book* to make books of their own to keep and read. We suggest that you keep extra sets of the stories in your classroom for the children to reread.

How to make a Decodable Takehome Book

1. Tear out the pages you need.

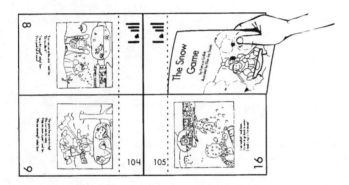

2. For 16-page stories, place pages 8 and 9, 6 and 11, 4 and 13, and 2 and 15 faceup.

or

2. For 8-page stories, place pages 4 and 5, and pages 2 and 7 faceup.

For 16-page book

3. Place the pages on top of each other in this order: pages 8 and 9, pages 6 and 11, pages 4 and 13, and pages 2 and 15.

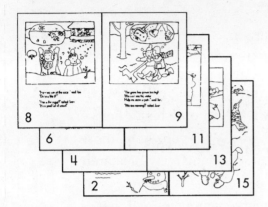

4. Fold along the center line.

5. Check to make sure the pages are in order.

6. Staple the pages along the fold.

For 8-page book

3. Place pages 4 and 5 on top of pages 2 and 7.

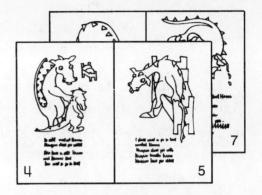

4. Fold along the center line.

5. Check to make sure the pages are in order.

6. Staple the pages along the fold.

Just to let you know...

A message from _____

Help your child discover the joy of independent reading with *SRA Open Court Reading*. From time to time your child will bring home his or her very own *Decodable Takehome Books* to share with you. With your help, these stories can give your child important reading practice and a joyful shared reading experience.

You may want to set aside a few minutes every evening to read these stories together. Here are some suggestions you may find helpful:

- Do not expect your child to read each story perfectly, but concentrate on sharing the book together.
- Participate by doing some of the reading.
- Talk about the stories as you read, give lots of encouragement, and watch as your child becomes more fluent throughout the year!

Learning to read takes lots of practice. Sharing these stories is one way that your child can gain that valuable practice. Encourage your child to keep the *Decodable Takehome Books* in a special place. This collection will make a library of books that your child can read and reread. Take the time to listen to your child read from his or her library. Just a few moments of shared reading each day can give your child the confidence needed to excel in reading.

Children who read every day come to think of reading as a pleasant, natural part of life. One way to inspire your child to read is to show that reading is an important part of your life by letting him or her see you reading books, magazines, newspapers, or any other materials. Another good way to show that you value reading is to share a *Decodable Takehome Book* with your child each day.

Successful reading experiences allow children to be proud of their new-found reading ability. Support your child with interest and enthusiasm about reading. You won't regret it!

SRA Open Court Reading

A Table

by Amy Goldman Koss
illustrated by Susanne DeMarco

A Division of The McGraw-Hill Companies
Columbus, Ohio

A

dog

A [ball] is on the [table].

ball table

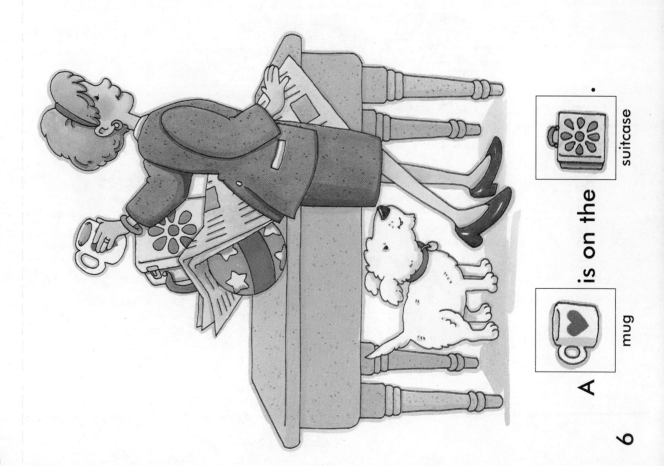

6

A [mug] is on the [suitcase].

mug suitcase

A  newspaper is on the ball .

A  suitcase is on the newspaper .

5

10

11

SRA Open Court Reading

The Egg

by Amy Goldman Koss
illustrated by Olivia Cole

SRA

A Division of The McGraw-Hill Companies

Columbus, Ohio

In the egg WAS a bird.

8

SRA/McGraw-Hill

A Division of The McGraw-Hill Companies

Copyright © 2000 by SRA/McGraw-Hill.

All rights reserved. Except as permitted under the United States Copyright Act, no part of this publication may be reproduced or distributed in any form or by any means, or stored in a database or retrieval system, without prior written permission from the publisher.

Printed in the United States of America.

Send all inquiries to:
SRA/McGraw-Hill
8787 Orion Place
Columbus, OH 43240-4027

In the [nest] is an [egg] .

nest

egg

3

On an island is a forest .

On the branch is a nest .

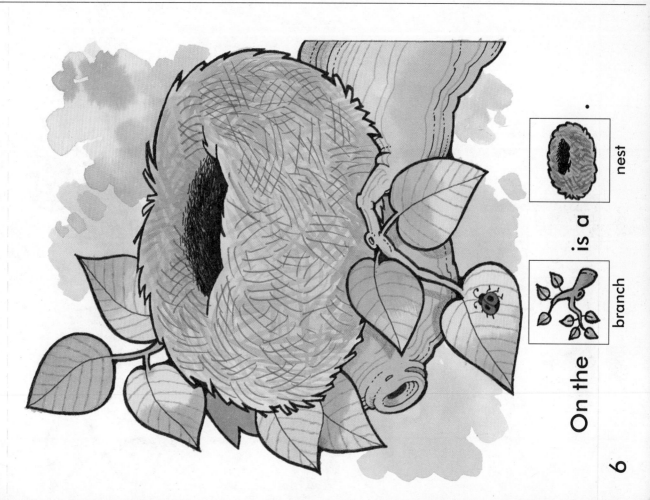

6

4

In the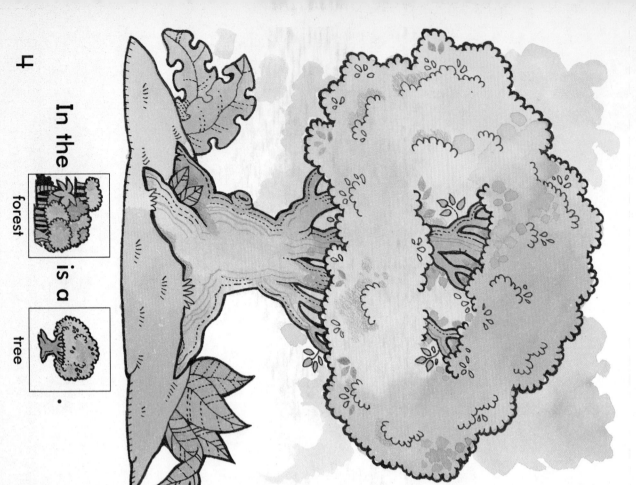

forest   tree

is a .

On the

tree   branch

is a .

5

SRA Open Court Reading

The Baby

by Amy Goldman Koss
illustrated by Sylvie Wickstrom

SRA

A Division of The McGraw-Hill Companies

Columbus, Ohio

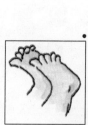

The 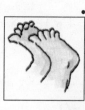 are on the 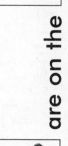 .

socks   feet

16

15

The [pants] are on the [legs] .

pants

legs

SRA
pen Court
Reading

The Cake

The  baby is in the  chair .

The  shirt is on the  arms .

Open Cou
Reading

4

The

cake

is on the

ear

.

The

socks

are on the

hands

.

13

18

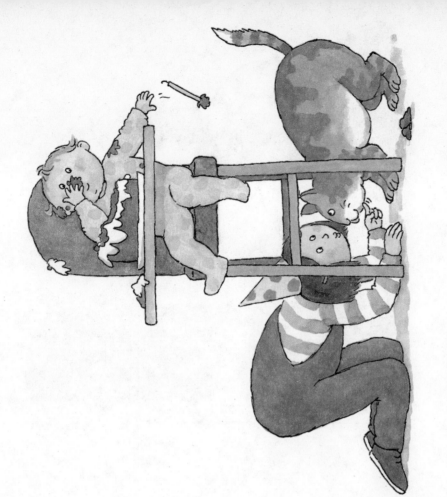

The  is on the .

cake   nose

19

The  are on the ... .

pants   arms

12

The

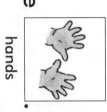

cake

is on the

hands

.

6

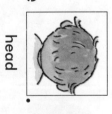

The Shirt

The

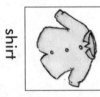

shirt

is on the

head

.

11

8

The

cake

is on the

girl

.

9

The

girl

is in the

tub

.

The

baby

is in the

tub

.

SRA
Open Court
Reading

What Mom Makes for Me

by Tim Paulson
illustrated by Olivia Cole

SRA

A Division of The McGraw-Hill Companies

Columbus, Ohio

23

8

2

SRA/McGraw-Hill

A Division of The McGraw-Hill Companies

Copyright © 2000 by SRA/McGraw-Hill.

Printed in the United States of America.

Send all inquiries to:
SRA/McGraw-Hill
8787 Orion Place
Columbus, OH 43240-4027

I will make a [Card] for [Mom].

7

24

25

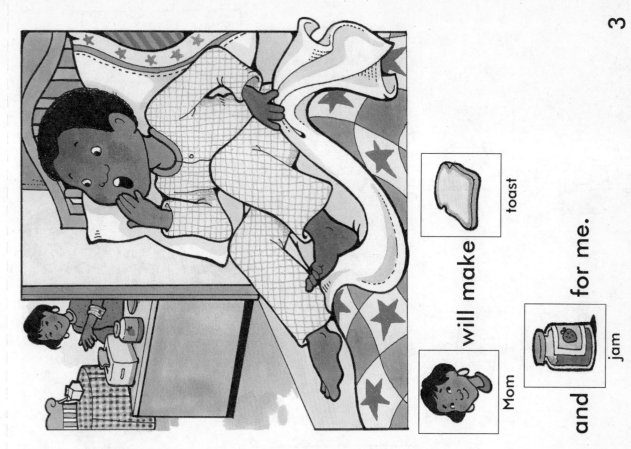

Mom will make toast and jam for me.

3

Where are the cookies?

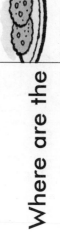

6

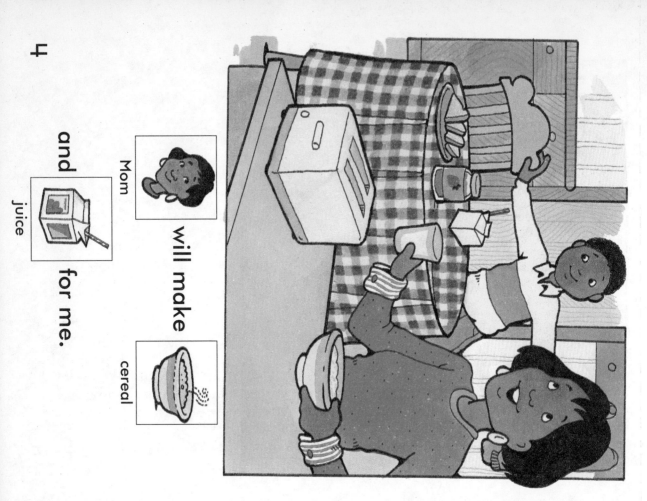

Mom will make

juice and for me.

cereal

After , will make

school Mom

cookies and for me.

milk

SRA
Open Cou
Reading

SRA Open Court Reading

The Hat

by Amy Goldman Koss
illustrated by Susanne DeMarco

SRA

A Division of The McGraw-Hill Companies

Columbus, Ohio

A ham!

27

8

SRA/McGraw-Hill

A Division of The McGraw-Hill Companies

Copyright © 2000 by SRA/McGraw-Hill.

All rights reserved. Except as permitted under the United States Copyright Act, no part of this publication may be reproduced or distributed in any form or by any means, or stored in a database or retrieval system, without prior written permission from the publisher.

Printed in the United States of America.

Send all inquiries to:
SRA/McGraw-Hill
8787 Orion Place
Columbus, OH 43240-4027

A ham in a hat?

Matt has a

hat

In the hat is a .

ham

In the hat is a

rabbit

In the hat is a

bird

SRA
Open Court
Reading

The Map

by Lucy Shepard
illustrated by Olivia Cole

SRA

A Division of *The McGraw-Hill Companies*

Columbus, Ohio

Pam's map!

8

31

Sam pats Pam's map.

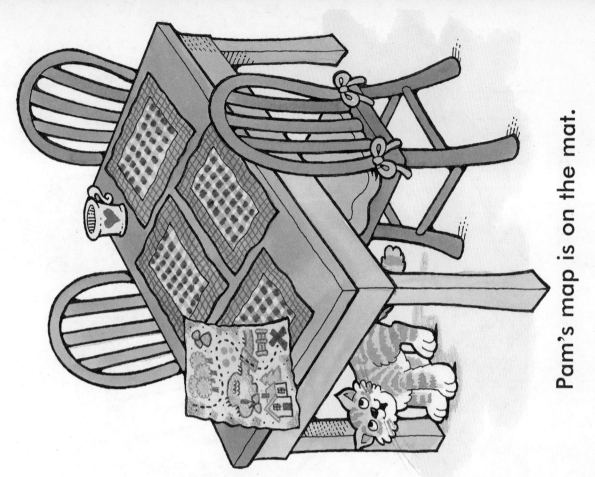

Pam's map is on the mat.

Sam taps Pam's map.

Open Cou
Reading

Pam taps the map.

Sam stamps on Pam's map.

SRA Open Court Reading

Hip

by Nancy Thomas
illustrated by Len Epstein

SRA

A Division of The McGraw-Hill Companies

Columbus, Ohio

Hip sits.

8

35

SRA/McGraw-Hill

A Division of The McGraw-Hill Companies

Copyright © 2000 by SRA/McGraw-Hill.

Send all inquiries to:
SRA/McGraw-Hill
8787 Orion Place
Columbus, OH 43240-4027

Hip hits his hat.

Hip has a hat.

Hip stamps.

Hip tips his hat.

Hip taps.

SRA
Open Court
Reading

by Nicole Michael
illustrated by Len Epstein

SRA

A Division of The McGraw-Hill Companies
Columbus, Ohio

Snap the Ant

Snap naps.

8

39

SRA/McGraw-Hill
A Division of The ***McGraw-Hill*** *Companies*

Printed in the United States of America.

Send all inquiries to:
SRA/McGraw-Hill
8787 Orion Place
Columbus, OH 43240-4027

Snap is by the pants.

Snap is an ant.

Snap sips.

Snap is on Pam's pan.

Snap has Pam's ham.

SRA
Open Court Reading

Nan's Family

by Anne and Robert O'Brien
illustrated by Linda Kelen

SRA
A Division of The McGraw-Hill Companies
Columbus, Ohio

I can!

Nan spins a tin pan!

16

43

2

SRA/McGraw-Hill

A Division of The McGraw-Hill Companies

Printed in the United States of America.

Send all inquiries to:
SRA/McGraw-Hill
8787 Orion Place
Columbus, OH 43240-4027

Can Nan spin tin pans?

15

On the Mat

Sam sits on his mat.

3

Nan hits and tips the tin pan.

14

4

I am on Sam!

Pat sits on Sam.

Tim spins his tin pan.

13

5

Tim sits on Pat.

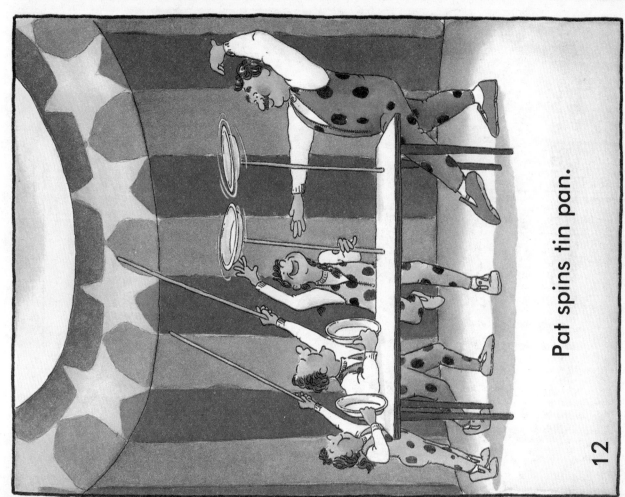

12

Pat spins tin pan.

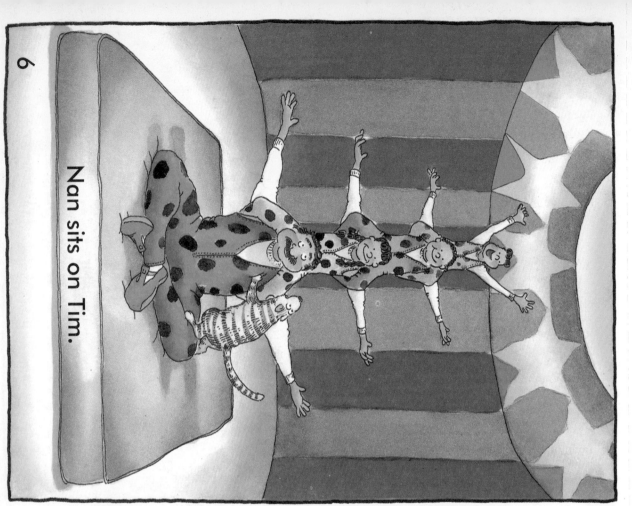

6

Nan sits on Tim.

The Pans

Sam has a tin pan.
Sam spins his pan.

11

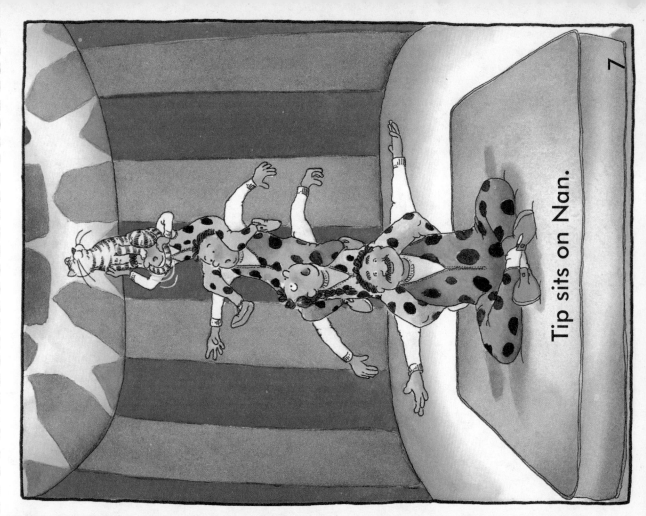

Tip sits on Nan.

7

10

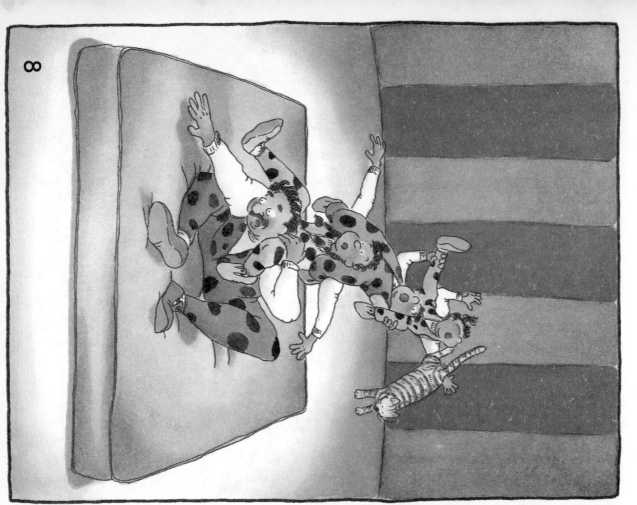

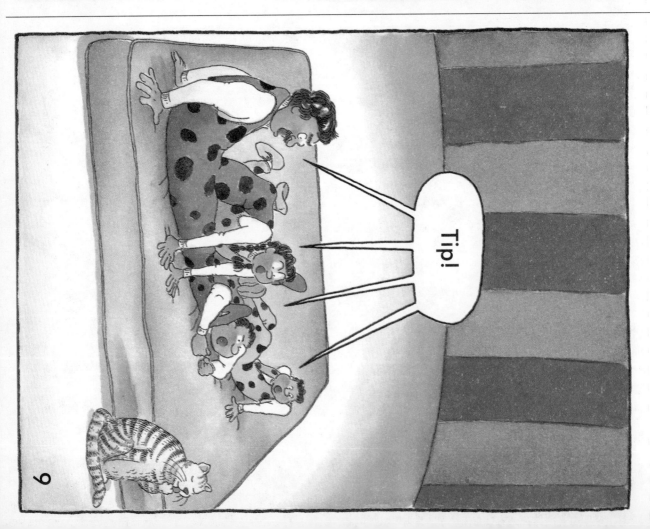

Open Court Reading

Tim Spins

by Anne O'Brien

illustrated by Susanne DeMarco

SRA

A Division of *The McGraw-Hill Companies*

Columbus, Ohio

51

Tim is sad.

8

SRA/McGraw-Hill

A Division of The McGraw-Hill Companies

Send all inquiries to:
SRA/McGraw-Hill
8787 Orion Place
Columbus, OH 43240-4027

Tim hits a pit...and sits.

Tim spins.

Tim spins his hat.

Tim dips.

Tim has a hat.

SRA Open Court Reading

The Spot

by Lucy Shepard
illustrated by Olivia Cole

A Division of The McGraw-Hill Companies

Columbus, Ohio

Dad mops and Mom pats the spot.

8

55

2

SRA/McGraw-Hill

A Division of The McGraw-Hill Companies

Copyright © 2000 by SRA/McGraw-Hill.

Printed in the United States of America.

Send all inquiries to:
SRA/McGraw-Hill
8787 Orion Place
Columbus, OH 43240-4027

Dad mops the spot.

7

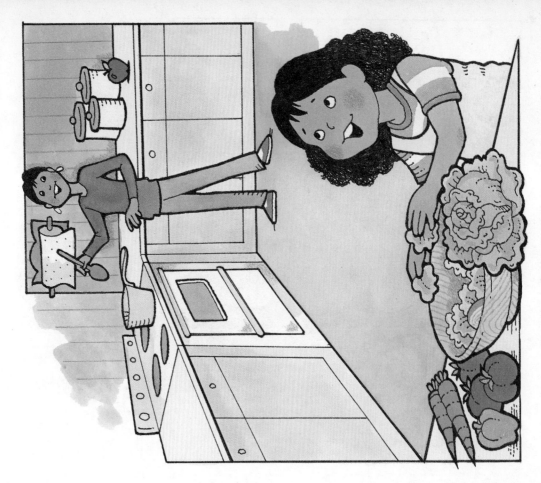

Mom has a pot.

3

Dad has his mop.

6

4

Mom's pot is hot.

Mom has a spot.

5

58

SRA
Open Court
Reading

Bob at Bat

by Nicole Michael
illustrated by Len Epstein

A Division of The McGraw-Hill Companies
Columbus, Ohio

Bob pants.

8

2

Bob bats.

7

Open Court
Reading

Bob is at bat.

3

Bob stands and nods.

6

Bob stamps.

Bob taps.

SRA Open Court Reading

The Cab

by Nancy James
illustrated by Len Epstein

SRA
A Division of The McGraw-Hill Companies
Columbus, Ohio

The cab stops and in hops Dan.

8

63

SRA/McGraw-Hill

A Division of The McGraw-Hill Companies

Copyright © 2000 by SRA/McGraw-Hill.

All rights reserved. Except as permitted under the United States Copyright Act, no part of this publication may be reproduced or distributed in any form or by any means, or stored in a database or retrieval system, without prior written permission from the publisher.

Printed in the United States of America.

Send all inquiries to:
SRA/McGraw-Hill
8787 Orion Place
Columbus, OH 43240-4027

Dan nods.

Dan stands.

3

The cab scats and Dan taps.

6

4

The cab spins past Dan.

5

Dan snaps.

SRA
Open Court
Reading

Sis the Cat

by Mike Dennison
illustrated by Susanne DeMarco

A Division of The McGraw-Hill Companies

Columbus, Ohio

I can sit with Sis and Dad.

16

SRA/McGraw-Hill

A Division of The McGraw-Hill Companies

Copyright © 2000 by SRA/McGraw-Hill.

All rights reserved. Except as permitted under the United States
Copyright Act, no part of this publication may be reproduced or
distributed in any form or by any means, or stored in a database
or retrieval system, without prior written permission from the
publisher.

Printed in the United States of America.

Send all inquiries to:
SRA/McGraw-Hill
8787 Orion Place
Columbus, OH 43240-4027

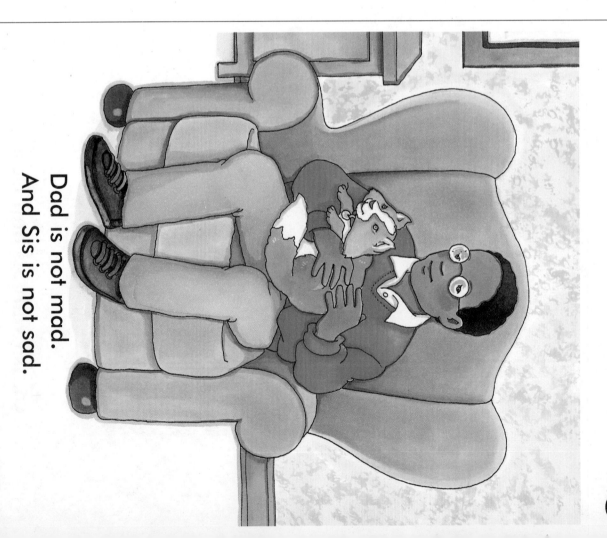

Dad is not mad.
And Sis is not sad.

Sis and Dad

There is Sis. Sis spins and stops on the mat.

3

Dad has Sis.
Sis sits on him.

14

Sis can sit.
Sis can nap.

I miss Sis.
Where is Sis?

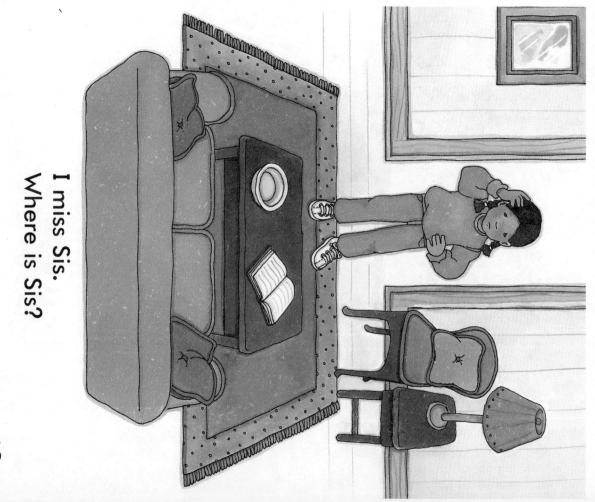

Sis can hit.
Sis can tap.

5

Is Sis with Sam and Pam?
No, Sis is not with Sam and Pam.

12

71

6

Sis taps the pans.
Sis hits the hats.

Is Sis in a tin pan?
Sis is not in a tin pan.

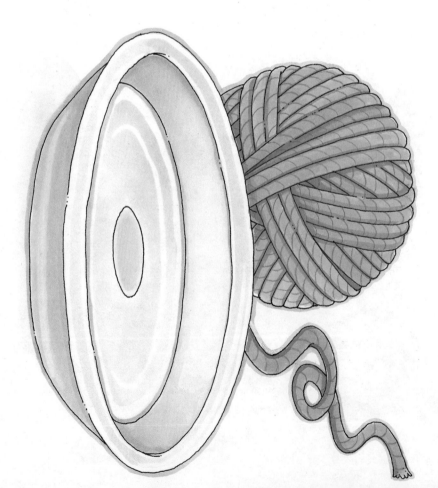

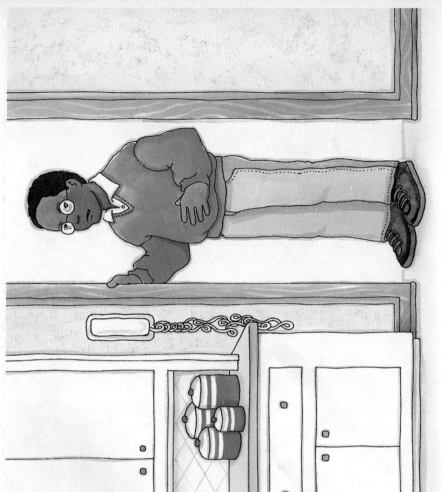

Dad is mad.
Scat, cat!

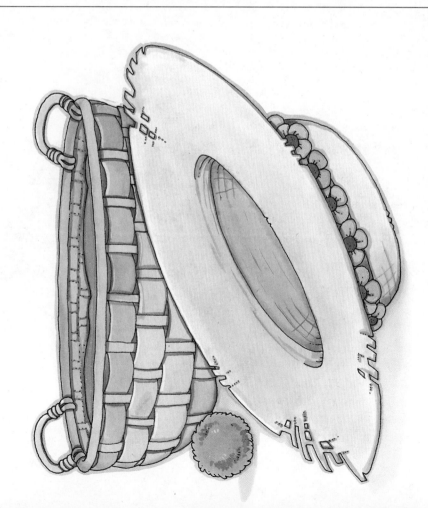

Is Sis in the hat?
Sis is not in the hat.

10

Where Is Sis?

Sis scats.
Where is Sis?

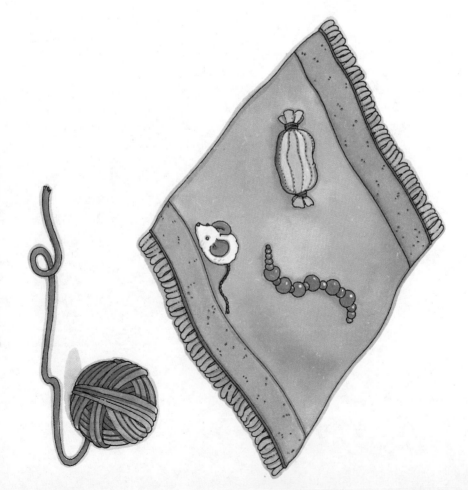

Is Sis on the mat?
Sis is not on the mat.

SRA Open Court Reading

Picnic

by Pam Matthews
illustrated by Olivia Cole

SRA

A Division of The McGraw-Hill Companies

Columbus, Ohio

Dad, Nick, and Pam picnic!

8

SRA/McGraw-Hill
A Division of The McGraw-Hill Companies

Copyright © 2000 by SRA/McGraw-Hill.

Printed in the United States of America.

Send all inquiries to:
SRA/McGraw-Hill
8787 Orion Place
Columbus, OH 43240-4027

Pam has the picnic sack.

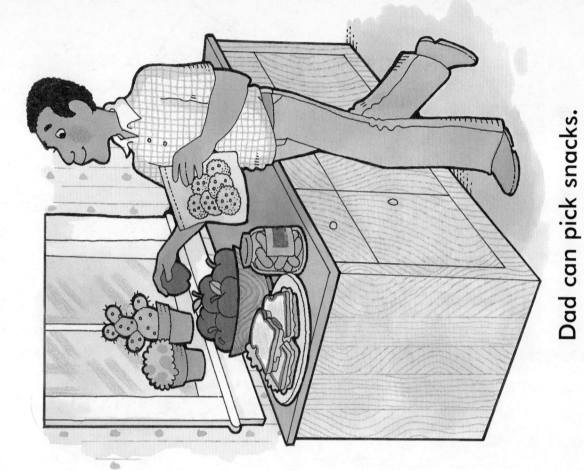

Dad can pick snacks.

3

Nick stands in sand.

6

Nick can pack maps.

4

Pam is in the back.

5

78

SRA
Open Court
Reading

Ron on the Run

by Alice Cary
illustrated by Olivia Cole

SRA

A Division of The McGraw-Hill Companies

Columbus, Ohio

83

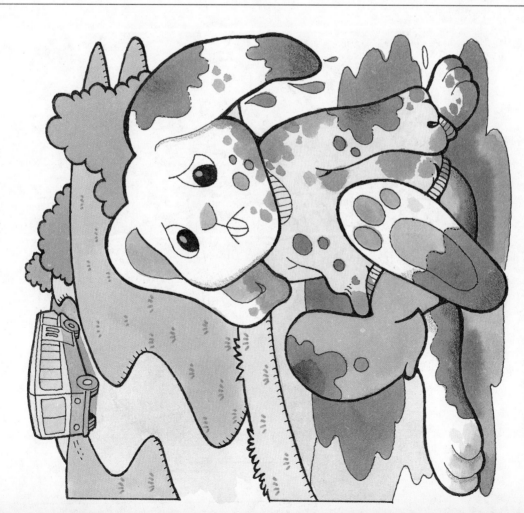

The bus runs on,
but Ron sits and does not run.

8

SRA/McGraw-Hill

A Division of The McGraw-Hill Companies

Ron runs for the bus.
The bus hits mud.
Ron sits in muck.

SRA Open Court Reading

The Bug

by Janet Klausner
illustrated by Deborah Colvin Borgo

SRA
A Division of The McGraw-Hill Companies
Columbus, Ohio

 : But is the bug big?

: Big bugs bump in big bags.

SRA/McGraw-Hill

A Division of The McGraw-Hill Companies

Copyright © 2000 by SRA/McGraw-Hill.

Printed in the United States of America.

Send all inquiries to:
SRA/McGraw-Hill
8787 Orion Place
Columbus, OH 43240-4027

2

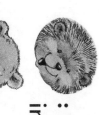

: Not the bag! Is a big bug in the big bag?

: A big bag has the big bug.

7

88

: What is in the bag?

: A bug.

: Yes. Is the bug in the bag big?

: It is a big bug bag.

6

4

: Is it big?

: The bug bag is big.

: No! Is the bug big?

: In the big bag?

5

90

Open Court Reading

SRA Open Court Reading

Sinbad the Pig

by Anne and Robert O'Brien
illustrated by Meg McLean

SRA
A Division of The McGraw-Hill Companies
Columbus, Ohio

"Sinbad has bad habits!" says Ann.

16

SRA/McGraw-Hill

A Division of The McGraw-Hill Companies

Copyright © 2000 by SRA/McGraw-Hill.

All rights reserved. Except as permitted under the United States Copyright Act, no part of this publication may be reproduced or distributed in any form or by any means, or stored in a database or retrieval system, without prior written permission from the publisher.

Printed in the United States of America.

Send all inquiries to:
SRA/McGraw-Hill
8787 Orion Place
Columbus, OH 43240-4027

Ann stamps.
Gramps grins.
Sinbad naps.

Sinbad Scats

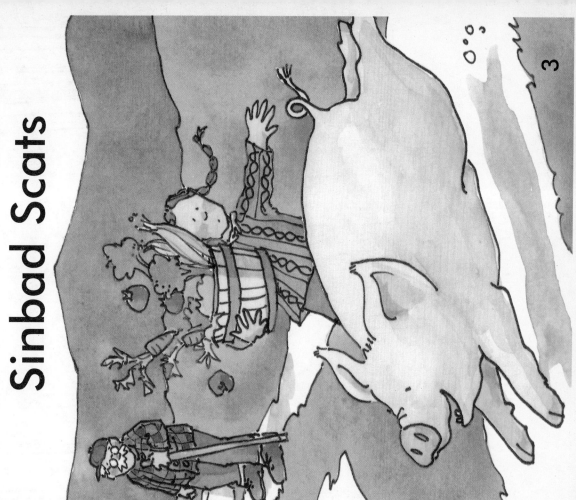

3

Ann trips on Sinbad.

14

4

Gramps and Ann have a big pig.

Sinbad stops and sits back.

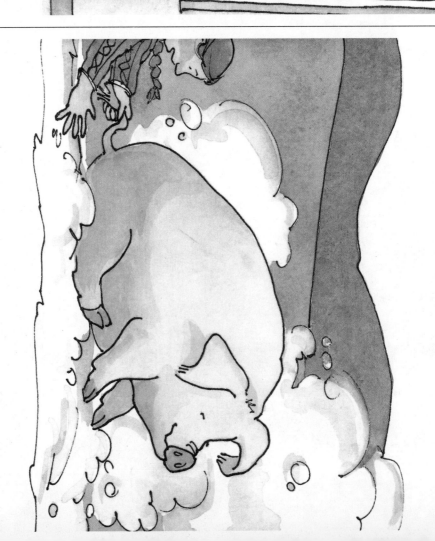

13

The pig is Sinbad.
Sinbad has bad habits.

5

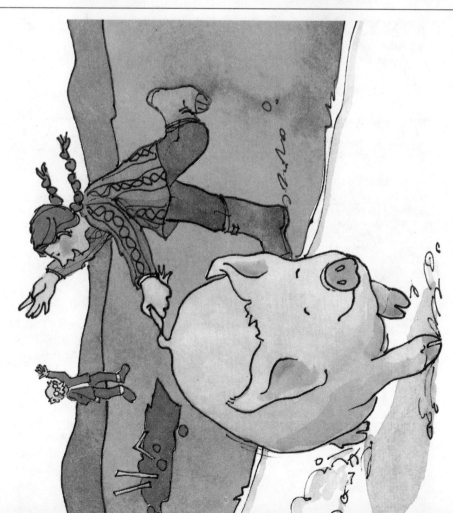

"I got him!" says Ann.

12

Sinbad bumps Gramps.

6

Ann grabs at Sinbad.
Gramps grins.

11

Gramps grabs at Sinbad.
Sinbad scats!

Sinbad runs.
He spins past Ann.

"Grab Sinbad, Ann!" says Gramps.

9

Sinbad and Ann

99

SRA **Open Court Reading**

Jan and Jack

by Amy Goldman Koss
illustrated by Olivia Cole

A Division of The McGraw-Hill Companies
Columbus, Ohio

"Jan, I am glad for snacks and a nap."
Jack sat and had his snacks.

8

SRA/McGraw-Hill

A Division of The McGraw-Hill Companies

Copyright © 2000 by SRA/McGraw-Hill.

All rights reserved. Except as permitted under the United States
Copyright Act, no part of this publication may be reproduced or
distributed in any form or by any means, or stored in a database
or retrieval system, without prior written permission from the
publisher.

Printed in the United States of America.

Send all inquiries to:
SRA/McGraw-Hill
8787 Orion Place
Columbus, OH 43240-4027

Jan tapped and nudged Jack.
"Jan, I had to sit and nap," said Jack.

3

Jan packed Jack's snack.
Jan put his snack in a jug.

Jack sat on the bridge.
Jack napped.

6

Jan tossed the jug in Jack's backpack.
Jan jogged up hills.
She jogged in grass and mud.

4

Jan hopped a big hedge
and jumped up on a bridge.

5

102

SRA
Open Court Reading

Brad's Ram

by Amy Goldman Koss
illustrated by Len Epstein

SRA

A Division of The McGraw-Hill Companies

Columbus, Ohio

Brad is a trim man.
He has a fat ram.
The ram has a fat hat.

8

SRA/McGraw-Hill

A Division of The McGraw-Hill Companies

Copyright © 2000 by SRA/McGraw-Hill.

All rights reserved. Except as permitted under the United States Copyright Act, no part of this publication may be reproduced or distributed in any form or by any means, or stored in a database or retrieval system, without prior written permission from the publisher.

Printed in the United States of America.

Send all inquiries to:
SRA/McGraw-Hill
8787 Orion Place
Columbus, OH 43240-4027

Snap! Brad's hat pops up!

Brad is a trim man.
Brad's trim hat fits him.
Brad has a fat ram.

Brad's ram tugs and puffs.

6

105

Brad's ram spins
and nabs his hat.
Brad is mad.
Brad nabs his hat.

PUFF PUFF

Brad pulls, puffs, and huffs.

SRA
Open Court
Reading

Jen's Pen

by Amy Goldman Koss
illustrated by Olivia Cole

SRA

A Division of *The McGraw-Hill Companies*

Columbus, Ohio

Ted pulls Jen out.
Ted pets Jen and feeds her bread.
"I will mend Jen's pen!" Ted says.
And Ted does mend Jen's pen.

8

Jen darts on top of the pen.
Jen trips and drops in a bucket.
"Jen is stuck and can't get up!"
laugh the horses.

SRA

Open Cou
Reading

SRA/McGraw-Hill

A Division of The McGraw-Hill Companies

Copyright © 2000 by SRA/McGraw-Hill.

Printed in the United States of America.

Send all inquiries to:
SRA/McGraw-Hill
8787 Orion Place
Columbus, OH 43240-4027

Ted has his hen in a pen.
Ted's hen is Jen.
Jen's pen is a mess.

3

"Jen is upset and is on the move!"
snort the pigs as Jen runs past.

6

4

Ted promises to mend Jen's pen.

"I'm fed up!" Jen sniffs.
"Ted said he would mend my pen,
but Ted did not mend it."

5

SRA Open Court Reading

Meg's Sled

by Dottie Raymer
illustrated by Deborah Colvin Borgo

SRA

A Division of The McGraw-Hill Companies

Columbus, Ohio

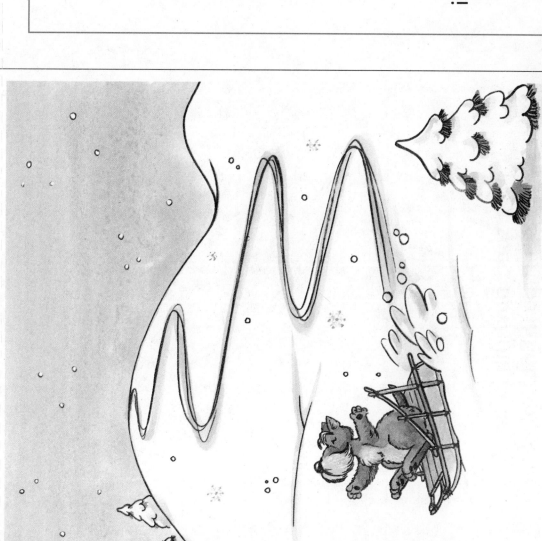

Meg and the sled sped on until seven.

8

SRA/McGraw-Hill

A Division of The McGraw-Hill Companies

Copyright © 2000 by SRA/McGraw-Hill.

All rights reserved. Except as permitted under the United States Copyright Act, no part of this publication may be reproduced or distributed in any form or by any means, or stored in a database or retrieval system, without prior written permission from the publisher.

Printed in the United States of America.

Send all inquiries to:
SRA/McGraw-Hill
8787 Orion Place
Columbus, OH 43240-4027

Meg sped past Bill Bulldog.
Meg sped past Bob Bobcat.
Meg sped past Helen Hen.

Meg pulled a sled up the hill.
Meg passed Helen Hen.
"Help me pull this sled," called Meg.
"I can't," said Helen Hen.

3

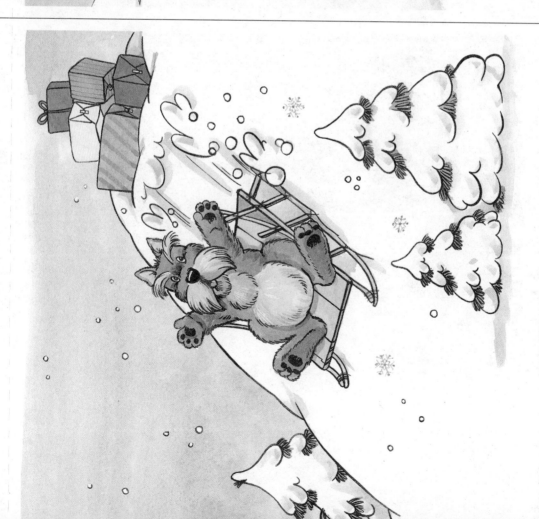

Meg got to hill's top.
Meg unpacked the sled and got on.

6

4

Meg pulled and pulled.
Meg passed Bob Bobcat.
"Help me pull this sled," called Meg.
"I can't," said Bob Bobcat.

Meg pulled and pulled.
She passed Bill Bulldog.
"Help me pull this sled," called Meg.
"I can't," said Bill Bulldog.

5

SRA Open Court Reading

Fred

by Marilyn Jager Adams
illustrated by Len Epstein

SRA
A Division of The McGraw-Hill Companies
Columbus, Ohio

"We can not sell a thing," grumbled Fred.

16

115

SRA/McGraw-Hill

A Division of The McGraw-Hill Companies

Send all inquiries to:
SRA/McGraw-Hill
8787 Orion Place
Columbus, OH 43240-4027

Tad dropped the brass lamp and ran fast.

Can I Help?

"Ham, Sam Clam?" called Fred.
"Not ham," clicked Sam Clam.

3

Tad rubbed the brass lamp.
"Puff!" it mumbled.

14

"Grab a top hat, Bill Bat," said Fred.
"No top hats!" snapped Bill Bat.

4

"Rub the brass lamp, Tad," Fred added.

13

"Test a dump truck, Dan Duck?" called Fred.
"No dump truck," directed Dan Duck.

5

"It brings me luck, Tad."
"Step up to the brass lamp."

12

"Jump in the jug, Ben Bug," said Fred.
"It's snug as a rug."
"No jug," blasted Ben Bug.

6

"Brass lamp?"

11

"Melted fudge, Judge Jed?" called Fred.
"Not melted fudge," said jumping Judge Jed.

7

Brass Lamp

"Have a brass lamp, Tad?" called Fred.

8

"Fig, Pat Pig?" called Fred.
"Not figs!" panted Pat Pig.

"I just can't sell things," Fred grumped.

9

123

SRA Open Court Reading

The Fox and His Box

by Marj Milano

illustrated by Deborah Colvin Borgo

SRA

A Division of The McGraw-Hill Companies

Columbus, Ohio

"Yes," grumbled Fox,
"and it did not trap you!"

8

SRA/McGraw-Hill

A Division of The McGraw-Hill Companies

Copyright © 2000 by SRA/McGraw-Hill.

All rights reserved. Except as permitted under the United States Copyright Act, no part of this publication may be reproduced or distributed in any form or by any means, or stored in a database or retrieval system, without prior written permission from the publisher.

Printed in the United States of America.

Send all inquiries to:
SRA/McGraw-Hill
8787 Orion Place
Columbus, OH 43240-4027

2

"It can trap rabbits?" said Rabbit.
"But I am a rapid rabbit! It can not
trap rapid rabbits!"

Rabbit and Fox sat on Fox's big box.

"You have a big box," said Rabbit.

"Yes!" snapped Fox. "It is a trap!"

3

"Can it trap an ox?" said Rabbit.

"It can not trap an ox," said Fox,

"but it can trap rabbits."

6

125

4

"Can it trap dogs?" said Rabbit.
"It can trap dogs," said Fox.

"Can it trap cats?" said Rabbit.
"It can trap cats," said Fox.

Open Court Reading

Zack the One-Man Band

by Diane Zaga
illustrated by Len Epstein

A Division of The McGraw-Hill Companies
Columbus, Ohio

"Do not fuss," added Zack.
"Grab tin pots! Grab small sticks!
Start a grand band!"
Zack and his band
got back on his red bus.

8

SRA/McGraw-Hill

A Division of The McGraw-Hill Companies

Copyright © 2000 by SRA/McGraw-Hill.

All rights reserved. Except as permitted under the United States Copyright Act, no part of this publication may be reproduced or distributed in any form or by any means, or stored in a database or retrieval system, without prior written permission from the publisher.

Printed in the United States of America.

Send all inquiries to:
SRA/McGraw-Hill
8787 Orion Place
Columbus, OH 43240-4027

2

Zack huffed and puffed.
"I must stop," he panted.

7

128

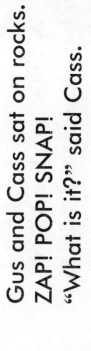

3

Gus and Cass sat on rocks.
ZAP! POP! SNAP!
"What is it?" said Cass.

BAM! BUZZ! BOP!
Zack's band started up.
"Zack, you are a grand band!" called Cass.

6

4

"It's a red bus. It has a man and a big brass band," said Gus.

The man on the red bus blasted, "I am Zack the One-Man Band, and here is my big brass band!"

5

131

SRA
Open Court Reading

Trash

by Amy Goldman Koss
illustrated by Len Epstein

SRA
A Division of The McGraw-Hill Companies
Columbus, Ohio

Mick put his trash stack in the small shed.

8

SRA/McGraw-Hill

A Division of The McGraw-Hill Companies

Copyright © 2000 by SRA/McGraw-Hill.

All rights reserved. Except as permitted under the United States Copyright Act, no part of this publication may be reproduced or distributed in any form or by any means, or stored in a database or retrieval system, without prior written permission from the publisher.

Printed in the United States of America.

Send all inquiries to:
SRA/McGraw-Hill
8787 Orion Place
Columbus, OH 43240-4027

five old comic books,
a crushed red drum set,
and half a smashed sled.

Mick had trash stacks:
dented and bent tin cans,

four fishnet strips,
torn flag scraps,

6

4

cut and split logs,
two smashed beds,

three cracked dishes,
small bits of crashed ships,

5

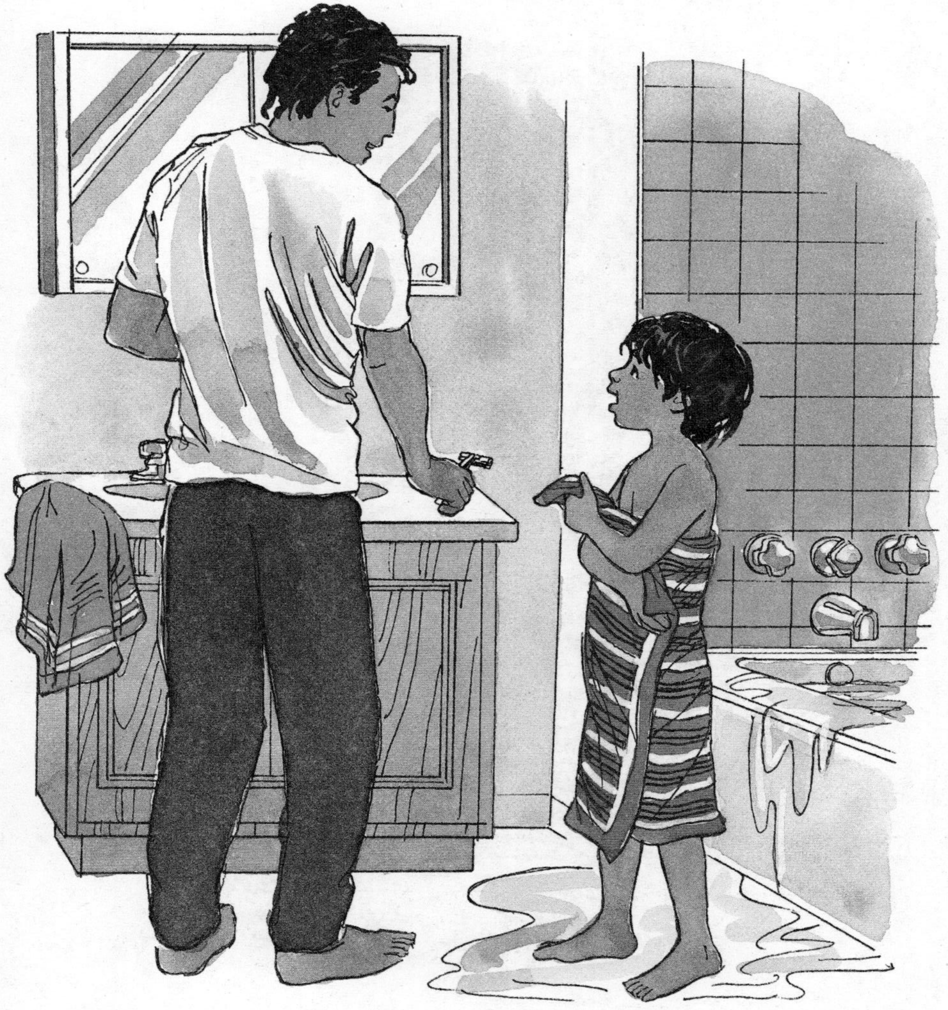

"All finished, Seth?" said Dad.
"Yes, Dad," said Seth. "All finished!"

SRA Open Court Reading

Seth's Bath

by Anne O'Brien
illustrated by Gary Undercuffler

SRA
A Division of The McGraw-Hill Companies
Columbus, Ohio

SRA/McGraw-Hill

A Division of The McGraw-Hill Companies

Send all inquiries to:
SRA/McGraw-Hill
8787 Orion Place
Columbus, OH 43240-4027

"Thick fog!
Abandon ship!"

Seth stepped into his bathtub.
"Must get to the ship!"

3

"The ship has thumped and hit big rocks.
Get the rafts!"

6

"Cast off!" called Seth.
"All hands on deck!"

"Rocks in the water!
Man the ship's masts!"

Open Court
Reading

SRA
Open Court
Reading

Panda Band

by Alice Cary
illustrated by Roz Schanzer

SRA

A Division of The McGraw-Hill Companies

Columbus, Ohio

Amanda Panda has Tom Cat's brass sax, a big band, and lots of fans. "You are tops!" Mom and Pop tell Amanda.

16

SRA/McGraw-Hill

A Division of The ***McGraw-Hill*** *Companies*

Copyright © 2000 by SRA/McGraw-Hill.

Printed in the United States of America.

Send all inquiries to:
SRA/McGraw-Hill
8787 Orion Place
Columbus, OH 43240-4027

2

Zack and Max drop in.
"Let's form a big band!" says Amanda Panda.

"Oh, no! More racket!" think Mom and Pop.

15

140

Amanda's Sax

"Sax racket!" mumbles Mom.

"Sax racket!" grumbles Pop.

14

4

Amanda Panda mops at
Tom Cat's Jazz Club.
She pushes a damp mop.

13

"Mom! Pop!" calls Amanda.
"I got Tom Cat's brass sax!"

142

Amanda stops.
"I can't stand this,"
Amanda sniffs.

Amanda's Band

SRA
Open Cou
Reading

6

"I am hot and a mess.
This job must stop!"

"I got Tom Cat's
brass sax!
I can drop the damp
mop and be tops!"

11

SRA
pen Court
Reading

Amanda gazes at Tom Cat and his brass sax.

7

"This brass sax?"
"Yes, this brass sax!"

10

"Tom Cat," Amanda grumbles,
"you do not have to mop.
You have a brass sax,
a big band, and lots of fans."

8

Tom Cat tosses
Amanda his brass sax.
"Hush," he tells Amanda Panda.
"I can fix things for you.
Have this brass sax!"

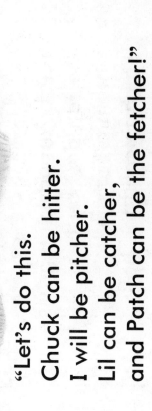

Open Court
Reading

Patch Gets the Ball

by Anne O'Brien
illustrated by Meryl Henderson

A Division of The McGraw-Hill Companies
Columbus, Ohio

147

"Let's do this.
Chuck can be hitter.
I will be pitcher.
Lil can be catcher,
and Patch can be the fetcher!"

SRA/McGraw-Hill

A Division of The McGraw-Hill Companies

Copyright © 2000 by SRA/McGraw-Hill.

Send all inquiries to:
SRA/McGraw-Hill
8787 Orion Place
Columbus, OH 43240-4027

Patch ran past tall grass.
He ran past bushes
and into the ditch.
Patch fetched the ball.

Lil, Midge, and Chuck
met at Chestnut Ridge Ball Park.
Midge pitched the ball,
and Lil hit it.
Midge ran after the ball and
tossed it to Chuck.

"Patch!" Midge called for her dog.
"Fetch the ball, Patch!"

6

"Let's switch," said Chuck.
Chuck was pitcher,
Midge was hitter, and
Lil was catcher.
Midge hit the pitched ball.
"I'll catch it!" called Chuck.

But the ball went past Chuck,
past tall grass, past bushes,
and landed in a ditch.

SRA
**Open Court
Reading**

Grab a Star

by Dottie Raymer
illustrated by Gary Undercuffler

SRA

A Division of The McGraw-Hill Companies

Columbus, Ohio

"I can catch stars!" said Max.

"Mom, you are smart!"

"Max," called Mom.
"This is a star you can catch!"

"Mom, are stars far off?" asked Max.
"Yes, Max," said Mom.
"Stars are far, far away."

Max mumbled, "Stars are so far.
I can't have stars."

4

"Mom, can I grab stars for fun?"
asked Max.
"Hmmm...grab stars for fun....,"
said Mom.

"Sit here, Max," added Mom.
"You can catch stars for fun."

5

155

Open Court Reading

Wendell's Pets

by Anne and Robert O'Brien
illustrated by Ellen Joy Sasaki

A Division of *The McGraw-Hill Companies*

Columbus, Ohio

"Here!" said Wendell.
"Next to me!"
And Wendell's pets sat next to him!

8

SRA/McGraw-Hill

A Division of The McGraw-Hill Companies

Copyright © 2000 by SRA/McGraw-Hill.

All rights reserved. Except as permitted under the United States Copyright Act, no part of this publication may be reproduced or distributed in any form or by any means, or stored in a database or retrieval system, without prior written permission from the publisher.

Printed in the United States of America.

Send all inquiries to:
SRA/McGraw-Hill
8787 Orion Place
Columbus, OH 43240-4027

Wendell's pets hopped, sat, and wiggled.
"Where will you put all the pets, Wendell?"
said Mr. Allen.

3

Wendell's Pets

When Wendell's pets went to his class,
his class was glad.
But Mr. Allen was not glad.

6

4

Wendell had lots of pets.
Wendell had his cat and his duck.

Wendell had his rabbit and his lizard.
Wendell had frogs and a tub for his bugs.

5

SRA
Open Court
Reading

Whir and Stir

by Patricia Griffith
illustrated by Len Epstein

SRA
A Division of The McGraw-Hill Companies
Columbus, Ohio

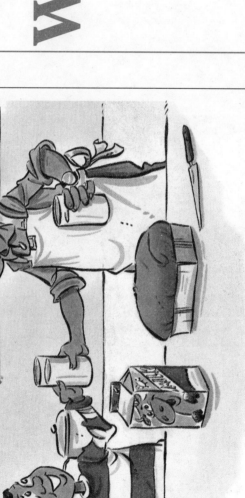

"Have a glass of fresh milk, Bert.
It turned into carrot bread,"
said Uncle Art.
"Carrot bread! Hurray!"

8

SRA/McGraw-Hill

A Division of The McGraw-Hill Companies

Copyright © 2000 by SRA/McGraw-Hill.

Printed in the United States of America.

Send all inquiries to:
SRA/McGraw-Hill
8787 Orion Place
Columbus, OH 43240-4027

2

"It was eggs and butter
and nuts and carrots.
What did it turn into, Uncle Art?
Is it finished?"

7

Uncle Art picked up his mixer.
"Pass the butter, Bert,"
said Uncle Art, "and let's stir in fresh milk."

Uncle Art put carrots and nuts
in his mixer.
WHIR!
"What is it?" wondered Bert.
"Pass the pan, Bert," said Uncle Art.
"We can put this batter in it."

4

Uncle Art put butter and milk
in his mixer.
WHIR!
"What is it?" wondered Bert.
"Hand me eggs, Bert," Uncle Art said,
"and let's stir in a little salt."

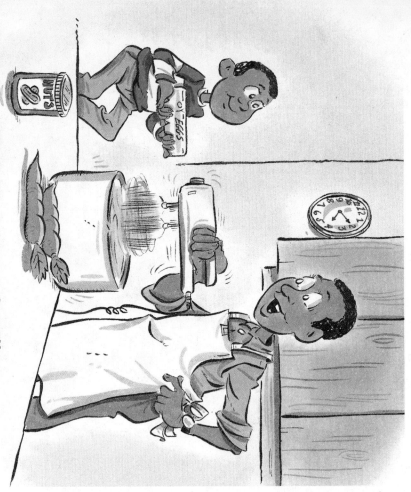

Uncle Art put eggs and salt
in his mixer.
WHIR!
"What is it?" wondered Bert.
"Pass the carrots, Bert,"
said Uncle Art.
"We will stir in nuts, too."

5

Open Court
Reading

Pick a Pet

by Meg Michael
illustrated by Susanne DeMarco

dPets to Pick...............3
A Pet Is Picked.........10

A Division of The McGraw-Hill Companies
Columbus, Ohio

: An octopus! Then you must tell him to keep his hands and arms off my stuff.

16

163

SRA/McGraw-Hill

A Division of The McGraw-Hill Companies

Copyright © 2000 by SRA/McGraw-Hill.

Printed in the United States of America.

Send all inquiries to:
SRA/McGraw-Hill
8787 Orion Place
Columbus, OH 43240-4027

: I will pick an octopus.
An octopus will fetch and whirl.

Pets to Pick

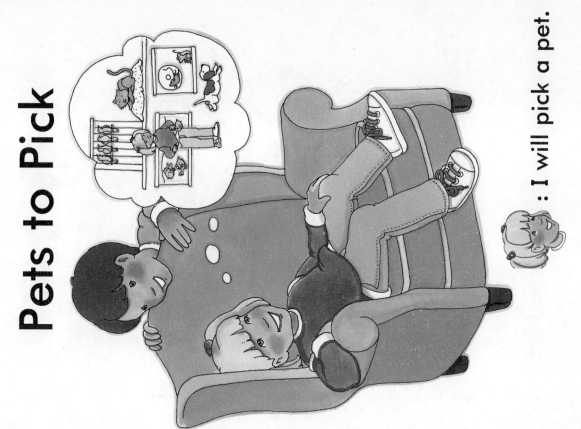

: I will pick a pet.

3

: Then what pet will you pick?

14

165

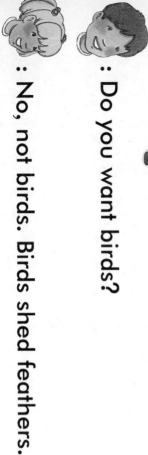

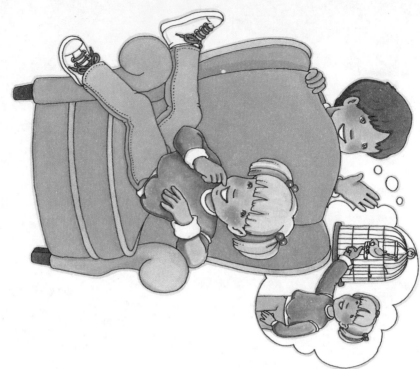

SRA
Open Cou
Reading

: Do you want birds?

: No, not birds. Birds shed feathers.

: Panthers are not good pets.
I will not pick birds or turtles
or fish. I will not pick chimps
or caterpillars or panthers.

: Then do you wish for turtles?
Turtles can swim.

: Not turtles.

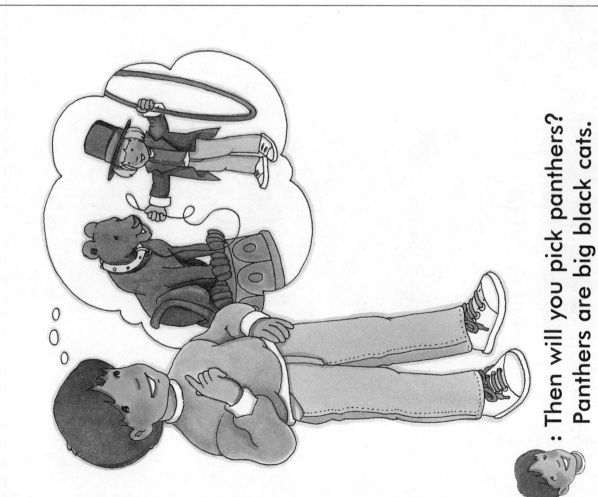

: Then will you pick panthers?
Panthers are big black cats.

12

6

: You do not wish for birds or turtles.
Will you pick fish?

: Caterpillars will not do.
I will not pick birds or turtles
or fish or chimps or caterpillars.

11

168

7

 : I will not pick fish or birds or turtles.

A Pet Is Picked

 : Perhaps you will pick caterpillars. Caterpillars will turn into moths.

10

8

: Perhaps you will pick chimps.
Chimps are fun.

: I will not pick chimps!
I will not pick birds or turtles
or fish or chimps.

9

Open Court Reading

My Trip

by Alice Cary
illustrated by Meryl Henderson

A Division of The McGraw-Hill Companies

Columbus, Ohio

171

I tramped on grass and trudged up hills.
But that fat skunk had a picnic lunch!

8

SRA/McGraw-Hill

A Division of The McGraw-Hill Companies

Copyright © 2000 by SRA/McGraw-Hill.

Printed in the United States of America.

Send all inquiries to:
SRA/McGraw-Hill
8787 Orion Place
Columbus, OH 43240-4027

I tracked that small skunk.
It sat nibbling on my picnic lunch!

For the trip, I packed park maps, snacks, and a jacket.
I tramped on grass and trudged up hills.

3

My backpack!
It had no picnic or snack!

6

173

4

I picked a flat spot in Birch Park.
I fixed my bag and rested.

I heard clicks and sharp snaps.
I sat up and kept watch.

5

Open Court
Reading

Hank the Crank

by Robert O'Brien
illustrated by Len Epstein

A Division of *The McGraw-Hill Companies*

Columbus, Ohio

Sheriff Long got the robber.
Farmer Ann got Hank.
Sheriff Long thanked Hank,
but the robber thanked Farmer Ann!

8

Hank started banging his head on
the robber's long leg.
Hank flung pebbles at the robber
and ran him up a lamp.

Hank was such a crank.
Hank was honking and hissing
as much as he could.
Hank honked at Farmer Ann.

3

A robber ran out of the bank
and jumped into Farmer Ann's van!
Hank banged on his box and tipped
it over. Hank honked and sprung
from his box.

6

4

"Hank, I think I'll sell you,"
said Farmer Ann.
Hank honked and hissed
at Farmer Ann.

Farmer Ann put Hank in a box
and put it in her van.
On her way to Mark's Market,
she stopped at a bank.

SRA
Open Court
Reading

Quarter Pond

by Stephan Queen
illustrated by Meryl Henderson

SRA
A Division of The McGraw-Hill Companies
Columbus, Ohio

179

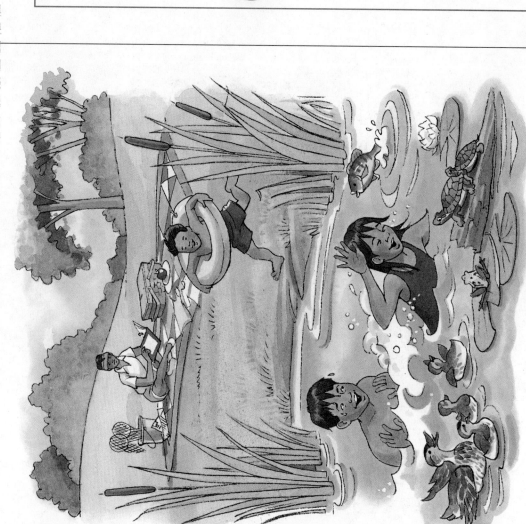
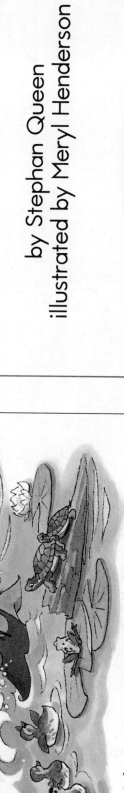

Kids can swim in
Quarter Pond, too!

8

SRA/McGraw-Hill

A Division of The McGraw-Hill Companies

Copyright © 2000 by SRA/McGraw-Hill.

Printed in the United States of America.

Send all inquiries to:
SRA/McGraw-Hill
8787 Orion Place
Columbus, OH 43240-4027

Kids squat by Quarter Pond, but
cannot catch the quick fish.

3

Lots of animals swim
in Quarter Pond.

Kids plan a picnic.
Mom puts her quilt
on the grass.

181

6

Squads of ducks quack
and quack.
Ducks do not quit and quack
until dark.

Fish squirt liquid at
bugs to catch them.
This bug is quick,
but this fish is quicker.

SRA
Open Court
Reading

The King of Purple

by Tim Paulson
illustrated by Kersti Frigell

SRA

A Division of The McGraw-Hill Companies

Columbus, Ohio

The men asked King Purple,
"Which one is best for you?
We do not understand.
First you loved purple, then black.
Next you wanted pink, then red."
An odd thing happened next.
"Perhaps this is best," said King
Purple, "after all."
Everyone chuckled and said, "Hurray!"

16

In dark red hills King Purple stopped at an art show. On this trip he got a red thing with springs. It went "zing." A red harp had strings that went "ping." He hit a red bell that went "ding dong."

King Purple liked purple.
His clothes were purple. His purple bed
had purple quilts. His rugs were purple.
His pets were purple, also.

3

The next morning, King Purple called
to his helpers again,
"I wish to be with things that are red!
Let's see red hills and red plants.
Somewhere on this trip we will see
pretty red birds."

14

In his beautiful garden King Purple walked and checked on his purple things. Purple buds, little purple yams, big purple squash, and a purple kumquat filled his garden.

4

The sun was setting when King Purple got back.

"Look up!" said King Purple.

King Purple squinted at the sun.

"That is not purple.

That is not black. That is not pink. I wish for things that are red."

13

King Purple went hunting on his purple yak.
He hunted purple birds, purple squirrels, and a purple bear.

5

King Purple went to the market.
He got some yarn and an umbrella.
King Purple got fun, fat pants!
All were pink!

12

In his backyard King Purple had purple plums, purple bananas, and purple lemons. King Purple picked a special purple berry for lunch!

6

When King Purple got up, he said, "Look up! What is that? That is not black. That is not purple. I like that a lot. I wish for things that are pink."

11

7

In King Purple's pond were purple fish and purple frogs. Quacking purple ducks and squirming purple squids swam in his pond!

King Purple went to a shop that had many black things.
They had black ink for pens and stamps.
King Purple got a black quill pen for a quarter.
King Purple put on a black mask.
Everyone laughed at him!
King Purple went back with his black things.
He went to bed and slept.

8

Everything in King Purple's Kingdom, from big to small, was purple. Purple, purple, purple, purple!

"There is too much purple. I am sick of just purple," said King Purple.
"Look up at that!" King Purple said to his men.
"That is not purple. I will get some things that are black."

195

SRA
Open Court
Reading

Gull and Crane

by Helen Byers

illustrated by Deborah Colvin Borgo

SRA

A Division of The McGraw-Hill Companies

Columbus, Ohio

Snake swam back across Lake Cape.

8

SRA/McGraw-Hill

A Division of The McGraw-Hill Companies

Copyright © 2000 by SRA/McGraw-Hill.

All rights reserved. Except as permitted under the United States Copyright Act, no part of this publication may be reproduced or distributed in any form or by any means, or stored in a database or retrieval system, without prior written permission from the publisher.

Printed in the United States of America.

Send all inquiries to:
SRA/McGraw-Hill
8787 Orion Place
Columbus, OH 43240-4027

Gull saw Snake, and she warned Crane. "Snake is in Lake Cape! Snake in Lake Cape!"

Gull and Crane are pals.
Gull and Crane did the same basic things.
Gull and Crane waded in Lake Cape.

3

Snake crossed Lake Cape.

6

4

Gull and Crane fished
together in Lake Cape.

Snake had a nest across Lake Cape.
He was mad at Crane and Gull.
They ate Snake's fish!

5